Colors

Brown

Nancy Harris

Heinemann Library
Chicago, Illinois

HEINEMANN-RAINTREE

TO ORDER:
☎ Call Customer Service (Toll-Free) **1-888-454-2279**
💻 Visit **heinemannraintree.com** to browse our catalog and order online.

©2008 Heinemann-Raintree
a division of Pearson Education Limited
Chicago, Illinois

Editorial: Rebecca Rissman
Design: Kimberly R. Miracle and Joanna Hinton-Malivoire
Photo Research: Tracy Cummins and Tracey Engel
Production: Duncan Gilbert

Originated by Dot
Printed and bound by South China Printing Company
The paper used to print this book comes from sustainable resources.

ISBN-13: 978-1-4329-1594-0 (hc)
ISBN-10: 1-4329-1594-0 (hc)
ISBN-13: 978-1-4329-1604-6 (pb)
ISBN-10: 1-4329-1604-1 (pb)

12 11 10 09 08
10 9 8 7 6 5 4 3 2 1

Library of Congress
Cataloging-in-Publication Data
Harris, Nancy, 1956-
  Brown / Nancy Harris.
    p. cm. -- (Colors) ꟿ7o2
Includes bibliographical references and index.
ISBN 978-1-4329-1594-0 (hc) -- ISBN 978-1-4329-1604-6 (pb) 1.
Brown--Juvenile literature. 2. Color--Juvenile literature. I. Title.
  QC495.5.H374 2008
    535.6--dc22
                    2008005612

Acknowledgments
The author and publisher are grateful to the following for permission to reproduce copyright material: ©Alamy **p. 9** (Holmes Garden Photos); ©Corbis **pp. 4** Top Left, **6, 22a** (Philip James Corwin), **19** (Tetra Images); ©istockphoto **pp. 5** Bottom Left (Moritz von Hacht), **5** Top Center (Viktor Neimanis), **5** Top Left, **18, 22c, 23b** (Lisa Remillard), **8** (Viktor Kitaykin), **12, 22b** (Steve Mcsweeny), **15** (Jim Jurica); ©Jupiter Images **p. 10** (Jim Wehtje); ©Shutterstock **pp. 4** Bottom Center (Elen), **4** Bottom Left (Maceofoto), **4** Bottom Right, **14, 23a** (clarence s lewis), **4** Top Right (beltsazar), **5** Bottom Center (Morozova Tatyana), **5** Bottom Right, **20, 22d** (Philip Lange), **5** Top Right, **7** (Noam Armonn), **11** (silvano audisio), **13** (Vova Pomortzeff), **16** (Larsek), **17** (misha shiyanov), **21** (Filip Fuxa); ©SuperStock **p. 4** Top Center (Photographers Choice RF).

Cover photograph reproduced with permission of ©Getty Images/Luis Castaneda Inc.

Back cover photograph reproduced with permission of Shutterstock/ WizData Inc.

The publishers would like to thank Nancy Harris for her assistance in the preparation of this book.

Every effort has been made to contact copyright holders of any material reproduced in this book. Any omissions will be rectified in subsequent printings if notice is given to the publisher.

Contents

Brown

Are all plants brown?

Are all animals brown?

Are all rocks brown?
Are all soils brown?

Plants

Some leaves are brown.

Some leaves are not brown.

Some stems are brown.

Some stems are not brown.

Some flowers are brown.

Some flowers are not brown.

Animals

Some feathers are brown.

Some feathers are not brown.

Some scales are brown.

Some scales are not brown.

Some fur is brown.

Some fur is not brown.

Rocks

Some rocks are brown.

Some rocks are not brown.

Soil

Some soil is brown.

Some soil is not brown.

What Have You Learned?

Some plants are brown.

Some animals are brown.

Some rocks are brown.

Some soils are brown.

Picture Glossary

 **scale** small plate that covers the body of some animals

 **soil** mix of small rocks and dead plants. Plants grow in soil.

Content Vocabulary for Teachers

body covering	outer layer, such as skin or scales, that protects an animal
color	depends on the light that an object reflects or absorbs

Index

Note to Parents and Teachers

Before reading:
Talk with children about colors. Explain that there are many different colors, and that each color has a name. Use a color wheel or other simple color chart to point to name each color. Then, ask children to make a list of the colors they can see. After they have completed their list, ask children to share their results.

After reading:
Take children on a nature or neighborhood walk. Ask them to list the different brown objects that they see on their walk. After the walk, ask children to graph the number of brown plants, rocks, buildings, and animals that they saw. Ask children which was the most frequent.

JAN   2010